For my soulmates, friendly and otherwise—
this is for you.
Thank you for lighting my fires and all the
ways you exist in the world that make you
deserving of every
work's dedication page.

for any reader who reads and resonates, you
hold a million little moments
in your care.

But mostly, this one is for me.

"Never be afraid to share your heart with others, you never know who needs it."

—Muriel Margaret via Instagram, December 22, 2018

Table of contents

lilac   8

orange   41

blue   62

yellow*   109

Disclaimer: Like any emotive art (all art), the muses and inspirations for the work in your hands vary. Some pieces started from real life events and eventually drew inspiration from stories in books and notes in a song and faces on screens. Inspiration is as plentiful in consumption as it is in experience. Everything in here is both real and conceptual. You'll find both alittle bit of me and a bit of the world on every page— and even I don't know which is which now.

FOR YOU...

You, the reader, who brought themselves to hold the words and world of my 15, 16, 17, 18 and 19 year old self in your hands.

if there's one thing I hope you get out of these million shining and devastating moments of my life— I hope you feel. I hope you feel happy, I hope you feel sad, joyful, and healing as I have grown to know it.

I hope you know how authentic expression can change, galvenize, and save your life.

I hope you know how much it means to me that you wanted to read the words of a young woman from the midwest.

I hope you embrace each part of your life, and know that there's nowhere to be except where you are. In your joy, in your darkness, in all of these moments, you'll find a silver lining cutting through the day to you. Even if that silver lining is only you.

There is strength in vulnerability,
there is healing in hurting,

and my dear,

you might not know yet,
but one thing's forsure:

You will be okay.

FROM ME..

Me, the girl with the pen through every era of her life. Whether in private or in public, in a classroom or bedroom— words and how they move are my comfort zone and my call to courage.

I come to you with my heart in my hand, both parts fear and courage and entirely made of the curiosity of fiery expression.

You and I, we are as much the same as we are different. We are finding our way through a life with no true guidelines or destination, looking for joy and discovering moments we never imagined (in the best and worst of ways).

From me, the overly emotional, sensitive, too-loud girl, the passionate, dedicated, expressive, and articulate woman.

To the you at the center of your being. Your truest self, and all the ways your heart ebbs and flows with the tides of your life. You are more than any mistake, any moment,

You are more than infinite

and here you are, holding my words in both hands.

More than anything, more than everything, I hope these pages make you feel human. I hope they let you know me, in my best and worst moments— before I knew who I was, and as I started wandering to figure it out.

Here I am, grateful for YOU. You should be too.

Enjoy. Love, Alyssa.

There are so many ways to lose yourself,
so many words to define you,
but half the time you'll find
you could pour out the dictionary and it
still
might come out wrong.

Beyond the mistakes,
the moments
the pain and the triumph..
who am I?
what fills me up with fire and light?
what do I dream about?

After stripping away the past, and all my attachments,
painfully and beautifully existing
immersed
in the present:

Where am I going?

i don't know yet

A collection of self-discovery by
Alyssa Burley

Places where
past is present...

He'd aged in the way a field on the outskirts of town would, coming back to the suburbs only after letting every bitter or warm aftertaste etch a few well-placed lines into his 19 year-old head. So many nights chasing the cinnamon of Fireball with nothing but the freedom of fleeing and the promise he'd never return.

Like clockwork he was back, stiff from remembrance and sticky with forgetting— the soil truly had shifted beneath him. One bestfriend and the boundary lines of town, they avoided each familiar gaze they'd grown so accustomed to forgetting and looked for ways to curb their regression into adolescent boredom.

Everything the pair sought had been seeking them all along, so when they found an app claiming to locate the small tears in time all around them, they were drawn in by the whim and the promise of adventure.

They trotted the town for days. They found bones in weary wooded clearings and found themselves deep in forests they'd never set foot in. They talked about all they'd found and forgotten in the year since they left and he came to the conclusion that he'd never come to terms with the inconsistency of life.

He looked at his bestfriend, knowing love would always live there, but failing to trust the way of the world in that it failed to show him kindness. The world he knew took the love between people and placed cell towers and asphalt between it, or let it waltz away into the arms of others— leaving him there to hold his own happiness, growing bleaker as he aged.

He could hardly see the road through the rain on the windshield, and his bestfriend's frame sank further into the leather of the passenger seat while trying to get the app to load.

"Got it!!"

His best friend held up the screen bearing new coordinates like a trophy, and he put the car in drive.

It took a few miles. He wasn't put off by the familiarity of the scenery because they'd been travelling in their hometown. They passed their old elementary school, smiling fondly at the beginnings of their friendship. They turned past the pool they played in as children, and slowed down the street where he'd enjoyed summer cookouts as a kid. Turning into an old alley more than familiar to him, the tinny voice of the gps rang out through the knowing air.

"Arrived."

They looked at one another, breath frozen in lungs locked in paralyzed frames. Then, they got out of the car and walked up to the destination the app had set out for them. They got out and walked up to the fence of the backyard of his childhood home. A new family lived there, but the swingset looked the same despite the time gone by, and he knew that they should leave soon before someone got creeped by the two boys standing at the back fence.

"bro, look."

His friend found something, poking out from under the leaves of an otherwise barren tree-line. An empty bottle of fireball sat in his best friend's palm, the red of the lid standing out from the gray of the day— walking him through every moment in the halls of his childhood, back up to the present.

He began to wonder if any of it was ever separate at all.

"Don't look back, I want to break free
If you'll never see 'em coming
you'll never have to hide.

Take my hand, take my everything
if we've only got a moment
give it to me now."

-Perfume Genius

It's you.
if you're looking for someone to show
you the love
that you lack
To light up your days and make you feel
again.
You
are the one.
Maybe you've been
walked over so many times you forgot
the steps it took back to the mirror to
look
at the beautiful safety to be found
in your reflection.
It's you.

its all in you to take yourself
past the frame on the wall that locks you
in like a prison
to the perceptions of others.
maybe you've been swept away in the
current of current events and can't
breathe but I can tell you
honestly,
romantically,
purely,
that you're the one.
you know deep down in you
what you need to breathe.
you've arrived.
it's you.

VULNERABLE

Don't take my loves from me
they deserve the length of
longevity
and every quiet morning with a
painted sky to see.

Don't take my life from me
sometimes its beautiful to bloom
beyond the fragility,

but please,

don't take my loves.
don't take my life.

punctuate my peace
and string up a thousand
obscured memories in my mind.

But please
leave my love and leave my life for
me.

HOPE

find your hope in the
knowledge
that there are a million cities
you've yet to set foot in,
14 billion pairs of eyes that
have yet
to know your face-
oceans to dive in,
lives to touch,
and new beginnings
everywhere
you
turn.
So why should you despair
at any circumstance?
instead of fear
and in spite—
of despair,
seek refuge in new eyes,
find shelter in towering skyscrapers
and when you fear for loneliness?
lay back and number the stars
because that is the number of ways
you have
to start new again.

you love as if the sky might open up and pour out
all the words you never say to me.

I know how to read the language now, 7 years
deep and down a few layers of understanding

But there are holes in every message that I just
can't seem to make out.

I know
because the years have taught me how you feel
and although it doesn't hurt me anymore

sometimes i wish you realized that the sky won't
open up and fill in all the holes your words leave
in my mind,

Divinity won't intervene
let me in or let me leave, I can't love a heart
leaving more holes in my mind
than gym floor
in my first pair of jeans.

Time passing by
but still I never move,
feelings don't die when you're
walking room to room.
It's hard to time travel when you
forget the leaves will ever change,
it's hard to trust the summer's sun
when nothing stays the same.
There's a flag on the wall where it
used to be bare,
it's hard for me to imagine that
nothing used to live there.
there's footsteps in the hall below
there's a million things i'll never
know.

it's hard to time travel when it's been
months since it moved,
the space between the past bridged
by me and you.

SOUL TIES

I'll be the words in your phone notes
the face of your 4am fantasy
and your definition of a city street corner.

I can be all these things for you, and I'll grace
every corner of your brain with a sense of longing
and a lingering "what if?"

when you left, I sat with a 3 am rain shower in
mind,
feeling that the only place it existed anymore was
in my head.

I'll be the AirBnB you bought but never blessed
and the subtle whispers of a magic that can only
be found in me. I'm the face of understanding and
your bearer of painful truth.

I know a spirit like yours will never find rest until
it finds the source of its newfound burning flame.

...CONTINUED

you are
my first 3am thunderstorm with the windows
wide and your fingertips heavy on my side,
and you're the lesson in ignoring my own
intuition.

I'll be the words, the face, the city corner in the
night, the rain shower, the Airbnb, the magic, the
understanding, the pain,

and the truth.

I'll be the feeling you never cease to search for in
all the doorways you come to grace.

I'll be all these pauses in time for you and more,
but I don't know if I'd ever want you to turn up at
my door,

At least until you can look at your pride,
and choose to care for me more.

I'm grasping at the seconds
of my passing life the way
people chase the sun
and
the futility of my efforts
leaves an ache in my chest
the way silence settles in
after a party's last drink
has been poured out.
In time my hours will
feel like seconds and I will
flicker and wither like
flowers in a frost in the late
hours of my life. I want to
hold on. I want the security
of these days that the
smiling sun is setting on.

Someone rewind my life so
I can feel it all once more.

Someone pull back my breath
I can't stand to watch it all
fade.

*(I didn't know it then, but sometimes
beginnings look a whole lot like endings)*

SHEDDING SKIN

there are snakes everywhere but
there are also souls, and I
am forgetting to recall
what comfort feels like.
and maybe,
that is why I lock up moments
of love in an iron fist
and each day,
convince myself to let it go,
coax myself into imagining
that i might find solid ground
again.

Shedding skin.
I know I'm not the girl they loved,
but I Am
the Woman I love now,
and it is the most bittersweet
tradeoff.

MAGNETISM

The 6am sun is rising in Toronto,
but my morning coffee's long
since run cold.
I think about you and the space
between us,
and how you'll wake to your
alarm—
no knowledge of the room you
sometimes rent in my head.
I should believe in fate,
and all these things that are
meant to be,
but I'd rather believe after being
there,
feeling 6am in Toronto,
as it is next to you.

diamond in the rough, you are the combination of
curiosity and the gravity of a thousand fiery riverbeds.
If I never find that kind of love in the pages of the past,
I know I found it in your face when it was day negative
ten and
you were still loving me like you already knew the soul
you observe now. We are the crippling laughter at the
margins of a tear faded page and the punchline of a
since-lost untimely joke—
but I never knew the pieces of connection to fall in line
so fast,
than when we opened our hearts to one another,
and never doubted that we would make it last.

But what can be learned from the touch of
your week long almost lover?
except that they mean that you are both
capable and worthy
of being observed with
both
love and longing
and you are one "almost"
closer
to the rest of your life.

I'm sharpening my scissors and
wearing my words,
and I'm learning to stand alone
even
when it burns.
I'll tape my mouth shut and
walk with my words,
because to protect my peace
I learned I'd have
to speak left of myself and allow
the universe to heal
what can never be right.

You,
are my satin sunset.
you are white wine and
euphoria and I don't
dive into drunkenness but
I could get high off of
the look in your eyes.

In time you will forget
this very moment you sit in. the elephant
in every room is that there's no way
to make the moment last.
Our moments are quick, and our lives
are fleeting and flying,
so if we can't quite grasp onto any of
the joy that lives in these moments—
what's the point?

The point is to be there. with all of you.
Is to hold them while they're here and
let them go when the next moment
calls.
let yesterday be yesterday, my dear.
Be here today.
Hold today and then let it go to
find a hundred thousand
glittering and devastating tomorrows.

Suddenly it's dawn and the stars still dance around
my head like last night's moonlit trainwreck is
something I would ever want to return to,

but when it's nothing like I imagined to dance in
the sun, the stars are all around me and I grasp at
them,

yet all that's left are red lights on your skin
and feet on darkened pavement
and the time I called you
pouring out tears like tomorrow would never come.

If the seasons change before I even blink to find my
footing and
everything I longed for looks more like a dream in
front of me than a life I grew to trust—

Suddenly it's all just shooting stars through the
night and a sparkling soul on the hood of my car,

if I never get that high for the present I think I'll
always go back in my mind
to the small moments in time when stars
poked through the sky

and the future was anything we said it could be.

sometimes the greatest gamble of
your day will be coaxing
yourself out from beneath the
covers and that
is enough.
If you've got enough faith in the day
that it might not fail you,
then you ought to have the same
faith
in yourself.

There are still evening showers in the
calm after the storm.
Breathe and let it wash away the trials of
tomorrow,
too much sunshine would dry you out
anyways.

You'll kiss me on streetcorners between the rush
and rise of every city sidewalk block,
and I'll let the spark in those devilish eyes light me
on fire in the evening's golden light.
Everyone who knows will see all the ways my heart
glows when I return with shoes in my hand and the
flushed cheeks of someone who has accepted the
greeting and getaway
of a kindred spirit.

I'll let myself feel that fire again, fuel for the fire
that fights me down the darkest of roads.
You'll kiss me goodbye in the morning and

I'll frame up the memory with question marks on
the walls of my mind,
but although I don't know,
I won't question.

Because there's enough fire in our eyes to keep me
glowing for a lifetime, even if
i never again step in your direction.

I have this image of life,
as it is from the passenger's seat
of
your best friend's car, street
lights washing over you in the
darkness of the night.
The quiet promise of a new
destination's euphoria
and hushed
3am conversations floating
through the magic air while our
friends sleep off the trials of the
day
arms hanging over one another
in the
back seat.

Running from the day break,
we live by the rush and the calm
of the night,
and these untapped moments
are the best of our lives.

suddenly without warning
life becomes less about waiting to
sleep
and more about waking up.
Warmth spreads across the skin
you used
to despise living in and you
become okay
with it,
with yourself.
Photographs where laughs paint
your face
leave you in disbelief.
There was always beauty there
where you
found joy beaming from your face
in that moment—
and you didn't pause to critique it.

After years of hurting, fighting,
crying,
suddenly without warning, life
becomes waking up.

When you fear for all the ones
you loved and let go,
remember always that the way
of the universe is in a complete
circle.
just as the earth orbits the sun,
and the moon circles the world,
the way of the universe is in a
complete circle,
and everything you release
will return
to you.

it just might not look how you think.

There are whispers of the past
in every silent room,
and memories like puzzle pieces
under the skin of everyone we
meet.

and when who we are
becomes what we survived,
the struggle is to remember—

that beyond the survival rests a
human heart
who is far more than the sum of
the
ways they kept living.

if you fall hard,
and they light you up
watch you burn down—
use your tears to put out the
flames,
and then stand tall.

Fire from the forked tongue of a
coward cannot burn you on its
own,
it's all a delusion.

unless you let them reach your
skin.

the misty morning of a cool June is all I am.
Many would like to define me as
the blood I have lost
or had on my hands.
A million negative moments
could've become me,
could
become me—
but I am not so frail as to condemn
myself the way the world would.
I am the moments in my life that
were most me, the seconds I
embraced myself in a way that cannot be carried,
from day to day.
The misty morning of a cool June is all I am.
All else can be let go.
it can be thought,
that you can be reduced to a fleeting
thought in another's mind.
But please remember that people
think many things.
Those thoughts have no power to
define you.
The misty morning of a cool June is all I am.

I'll find you in another life.
in a universe no textbooks
 talk about, we'll learn all
the same lessons of loss
and love we thought we'd
escape when fate stole us
from the world we wear
each day.

Don't forget how your heart
fills up and flies
with the hello after every goodbye
while your feet still stand firmly on the pavement.
I know life can be redundant,
and like washers gray your clothes—
time can mute the colors of a vibrant life,
if you don't hold fast to the moments your heart takes
flight.
Whatever fills your heart with helium and lets it fly
away—
grab it and carry it with you through all the days of
your life.

I long for you,
hair pulled back
so I can look in
those eyes.

I long for you.
I catch flashes in
a golden montage
of a you without
heartache,
the you that would
sit by me and let the
world pass by all
around us.

I long for you.
In sibling cities miles away,
I overlook the space
and all the pitfalls,
and all I do
is long for you.

but if there's freedom anywhere in this
universe for a spirit like mine,
it won't come in an instant.
It'll heal and become real with time.

Excerpt.

eyes that say yes, I'm living in a dozen
different cascading memories with you,
jumping and falling down every city
street into the magnetism
of your smile.

She wants the snow to stick
around this year,
kind of the way the memories of
her living in it as a kid do.
For some reason tonight it breaks
my heart that I can't blow
snowflakes into her air,
skip rocks on the east river
or fly down an icy hill with the
wind in our hair.

She wants the snow to stick
around this year, and I hate the
cold but I love to watch her face
light up with an enthusiasm she's
kept far longer than I could.

I'd paint every sky blue for her
and in my mind I'll always be
swimming in the pools of my
childhood, because somehow she
created an adventure for me there

that I'll always be hoping to give
back to her.

I hate the cold,
but I want the snow to stick
around this year.

and maybe for us
our new beginning
is our ending as well.

A. BURLEY

"When I dare to be powerful,
to use my strength in service of my vision,
then it becomes less and less
important whether I am afraid."

-Audre Lorde

and beneath the cold you'll find us
burning a hole through
the darkness
because even if we burned down
the dark walls of a system that
failed us
we would still be there
smiling
dancing as the ashes crash down
at our feet.

the greatest propaganda is the kind
that convinces you that someone
is any less human
than yourself.

we carry around our universes as if
the universe doesn't wake up to
meet our eyes every morning.
I often wonder if reality gets tired
of watching us forget to tend to her
while we immerse ourselves in the
reality someone miles away created
for us,

Can't we just live in the real world for
awhile?

Tending to the voices of the world is
draining when our cohesive message is
that of our own brokenness.

Can't we just live in the real world for
awhile?
The place where you don't have to
convince yourself you're worth it,
where you can decide how you feel,
where you aren't confronted with the
noisy chaos of a million misguided
hearts the moment your eyes fly open
from your dreams.

How do we decide what's real in this
muddled air?
The quiet's losing it's way and our
minds are blanketed in dust without
it.

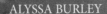
ALYSSA BURLEY

I see it in your tired eyes
you've seen more gore than glory on
this everlasting rollercoaster ride.
the days speak in tones of gray and
you feel like you're wasting away into
the darkness of a world so bleak,
but there are still trees left to save in
the Amazon
and untouched beaches by the sea—
if one person has found recovery,
there is hope for you and me

Politicians are employed to please.
I am not a politician. I am 15,
and my blood boils when you raise your voice,
and forget
to raise the standard
for the content of your argument.
You're loud with your ignorance and
silent
about your mistakes, but when
you raise your voice,
I see with the tunnel vision in your mind and
suddenly—

I'm a politician conducting my choir of
a crowd
of people who believe against the
fallacy of their own beliefs with such
a certainty
I might think them to be God themself.
But the fallacy in your belief perpetuates the
suffering of another,
and your ignorance rips me to the core.
Politicians are employed to please.
I am neither employed
nor respected by you,
and i will never again shrink to please
the unimpressed,
the misinformed,
you.

visionary is a great title,
until your mind gets so caught
building the future,
your hands forget to pause long
enough to enjoy the future
that exists today.

SKIN...

you cannot wreak havoc
under a woman's skin and
in her heart.
you cannot use her
and abuse her as if she
was somehow lesser
because God bestowed
her with beauty.
Abuse and abandonment
aren't two separate things,
but trauma is human today and darkness
covers those who spread it.

...CONTINUED

Recognize her simple humanity and
refuse to infringe upon her
faithfulness, because stealing light
from someone's eyes is not your
power nor your right,
but a woman's ability to feel safe,
on the sidewalk, in the workplace, in
your room—
is both her right
and your duty.

There are tears across the rooms of your
childhood and a home across the globe
with a heart and soul beating
just for you—
but you've blazed your way through
a world you didn't feel belonged to you
and

the sum of your parts transcends the
boundaries of faultlines, of constructs,
of youth and of trauma,

and somehow each time you smile
you're there
rising up each and every time,
burning a hole through every darkness
like you knew who you'd become before
the seasons even dared to change.

(excerpt)

SLEEPING IN SUBURBIA

there's a place past the valley that is only ever
half-awake, or maybe more so
half
caught up in their own dream.

Before the day suburbia swallowed me, I could walk around strung
high about the neck by a noose woven of outside
expectations and inside aspirations, and never take a single syllable of
it seriously. I was there to witness, to play the part, but if I was aware—
it could never touch me, right?

I was never going to let it far enough under my skin to burn the
 precious parts of myself that I kept stowed away from the world.

the tumult of a town with a dome connecting it's horizons is the
seductiveness of the reality it
perpetuates between its boundary lines.

if you've never known another place,
you hold the mirror of flaw to yourself instead of the status quo and
stumble into the daydream you scoffed so heavily at.
When you let your guard down, you know what it means to live in a
sleepy little town.
and one day looking back,

you'll know that you let yourself down.

Slow dancing with the devil
is a hobby of mine.
it's painful how beautiful he makes it
look
when his words smile at you.

I lay my head on his burning chest,
but when you're cold
you can't feel the heat until it burns
straight through you.

and I'll dance on my own
and let the rhythm of my own
mangled heart mend the burns of trial
and error,
and I will forget that the devil wears a
halo
when he says
sorry, and dresses in white,
when he plans to stay again.

he told her she wasn't enough.
he sent out attacks with the intent
to strip the voice from her lips
like
it ever belonged to him to begin
with.
he thought she wasn't enough,
and thus is how she lived.
Darkness was the road she
walked
until the day the sky dawned on
her power and
the sun set on her dependence.
She now
demands
her worth.

the rays illuminated her own form
through the dark
and suddenly it became clear.

she was not his cruelty,
and was never the mercilessness of
a man
with no regard for the heart in her
chest.

she still spoke with the same voice,
and touched with the same hands.
she was still here,
but she was now herself.

she was more than enough.
and thus, is how she lived.

*(You've always been far more
than you ever imagined)*

I am both the bleeding heart
with a worn doormat and
high hopes for the abuser
with a beautiful grin
and I am
the iron clad fortress with
a knack for floating past
the fakes and fools,
loving them but remaining
unscathed, safe,
in a fortress built by my own
bloodied hands from the
past.

But the heart still bleeds
in the walls of her own
castle when love looks
like war games and
indecision turns to
termination.

I'm both the solace in
knowing that alignment
means joy and the
agonizing beauty in the
eyes of the lesson you
prayed to spend forever
learning.

54

That look in your eyes
sounds like
these streets that never change
and sleepy lives with
lips
like a faulty noose
but I can see you running
that behind the gift of simplicity
you long to draw back
this suburban curtain
and shine your light on a life
that doesn't feel
like suffocating.

Wallflowers don't always wear the mold of a misfit.
Sometimes they look like perfection and
embody the grace and humor of those who spent
their childhoods raised up like hands in a church.
So much so that nobody looks further than the
glittering facade of a beautiful face and carefully
crafted picture show to see the depth
of understanding and pain it requires
to mesh so beautifully with all the shifting
walks
of people from different lives.

It's easy to wonder how life got
this way,
 how you became so messy or
began feeling so broken.
In counting the ways your life
became something you never
wanted it to be,
you're also realizing that at any
moment it can become what you
never expected it to be.

So even while you despair at the
pain of the present, draw some
parenthesis in your mind and
remember your life can be
summed up in three words:
(Subject to Change)

I know I cannot rationalize the
thoughts of an entire world,
but I can conquer all
the obstacles of my own.

*We can change the worlds we can
touch.*

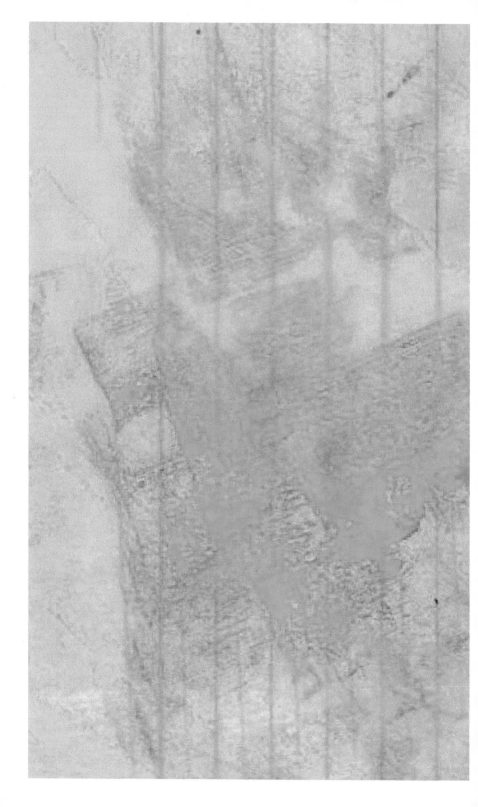

We've washed our hands of yesterday's
grievances,
but we start each day the same way.
Forgetting,
and being reminded day
after day, after day

A. BURLEY

"Grief and resilience live together."

-Michelle Obama

I am made of fire
and of fight, and of
independence
but some days it seems
a mere thought would
be enough
to drown me.
Is needing a lifeboat
weakness—
if you never ask for
one?

A. BURLEY

and i'll go back to a city so far from
you.
Where you don't even think twice
about me.
but I will about you.
I always do.

Most of us spend
our whole lives
learning the lessons of
a past life and
what a shame it is that,
what looks like burning
bridges is actually
breaking free.

but in my head i'm letting go
of your hand and
although my fingers are
still outstretched
they're falling through
space and time
back to someone who
respects me without possession.
falling down through every moment
back
to myself.

in the early hours
it's easy to forget
that 4am is not nearly
long enough
to face the demons
of an entire lifetime.

eventually the irony of it all fades and I'm left
here on this sidewalk in the city
giving an empty gaze to the masses and feeling the re-
sult of everything that's come to pass seeping in on me.

So I'll fall for the first impressions.
I'll walk backwards and I'll watch the old movies,
forgetting to remember the lessons of my past life.

The songs on the radio will change and the seasons will
too,
your face will fade
but our ghosts still dance around the parking lots of my
hometown and a shooting star
still hangs frozen over a still-life of our first moments.

I dance backwards and forget to remember the joy that
I found in you, I drink up the newness of nights under
bar lights and toasts
to things that won't matter when day breaks.

But here's to the hope that one day I'll fall for more than
a person's fabulous first fifteen. That they'll come in
with flying colors and keep me hooked with
consistency
that I'll look at them and stride forwards out of this
backward spiral,
and paint over the mundane daybreak with a 100
shades of golden sincerity.

I DON'T KNOW YET

I've witnessed the few
who have found themselves in love with
me.
I have seen it in their eyes,
smelled it in the flowers,
read it in the words,
felt it in the way they touch— with hand
and
without.
And most tragically,
i have seen, I have felt,
I have witnessed
the way time changes their hearts,
the way time taints their touch,
the way time changes them and
takes them
away.

(from the journal of a 15 year-old me, funny enough)

you got too high
off the idea of me
then blamed me
because it hurt
when you fell.

some days I am a puzzle piece that has no
complementary pieces.
I am always,
diving in head first,
but only waist deep.
Falling so far for people, but
only half comfortable.
Is it my jagged edges, or the world—
or both
that keep me stuck in this cycle?

sometimes i want to call you on nights like
these.
Your voice has a gravity rivaling that of my
demons,

except maybe more tasteful.
except maybe,
I am all pride in my moments of pain and how
do you tell someone who sparkles that lately all
you've done is rain?

It's a strange dichotomy to want and to waste
away,

but if i smile when i think of you now could it
draw back the yearning to land by you before I
fall?

So I'll sit on the edge of my late summer's
secret,
a heart in hand and a call I just can't quite keep.

and i know one day I'll be
tracing the ghost of your
embrace around my heart
so forgive me if i tell
you i love you too often
or stare at you a little
too long, almost as if
trying to burn
the image of you, happy
and healthy— into
my heart
for a day when it's
needed most

ALYSSA BURLEY

a patch once covered
the holes in your clothes
the wounds found in falling and skinned
knees
found healing in bandaids and kisses. But
I'm 16 now and a long time ago I came to
the sobering realization that the worst
wounds are deep under my skin, and

I cover them in conversation and
diversion but
to my dismay—

these holes don't heal quite the way my
knees did,
and grocery stores don't sell bandaids for
the soul.

(But they do sell journals and music, and house the
smiles of strangers.
i didn't know it then but
you'll be alright)

i hate the curb lane but I'm chasing tail lights
rushing home from you.
Overnight will never be enough and I may
never become your forever like we planned
but at least
there's someone out in the world that makes
me feel that way,
even if life planned it
so that I'd have to be tracing the shape of
your absence in my life
day after day
after day.

(some voids aren't meant to be filled)

Don't compromise your future while wandering the long-since expired hallways of your past.

Loss bred doubt in the very veins
meant to keep me alive.
it's hard to remember that I am
more
than what I am told.

and you stand there, the ache in your
chest,
watching your heart walk out the door.
But you just stand.
you don't chase or call out.
you hurt,
but you love yourself enough to let it
leave
because if anything in this life was
meant for you
there's absolutely nothin you could do
to prevent it from being.

Text me once in a blue moon,
Remind me that you love me.
that somewhere in the chaos of the world
there's permanence
in a heart always pointed towards me.

Give and take away
life became a cruel guessing game.
don't give me the trailer
but not the film.
don't give me the heart
but not the person
who goes with it

(all these spaces between you and I)

Victim to my own indecision
I'm counting down all the
reasons you'll never see me
again, as if the proper way to
find closure was chasing the
pain around my bedroom
like it held all the answers.
So I let a 5 year old balloon
disappear into the atmosphere
of my life,
I shot my message into the
void and I asked for the wisdom
to fill it and
its nothing
like I wanted it to be.

all there's left to do now
is let you fade.

Most people are only willing to give in
vulnerability that which they're given
but if its too early or by surprise
the prospect of a recoil is so great, that
the gravity of vulnerability shifts from
comfort to fear
and words echo through the hallways
of your mind.

Because people can only love you with
the things you've shown them
but once you give you can't decide what
you get back
and most of us are still healing from the
failed gifts of connections in our past,

so much so that digging deep with
someone new
seems an unworthy task.

I scan faces of strangers looking
for familiarity
as if the countenance of comfort
could truly bring me home.

I search the hearts of friends longing
for loyalty
as if the gravity of a true friend could even
pull me back to myself.

The only map I ever found was in
a mirror
as if reflecting on history
could ever bring me to a place
where I am home.
If I can't look me in the eye,
I'll never expect someone to see past them.

When did I start watching star signs and looking
to internet strangers
to give me hope
to give me a sign
to tell me I'm not a fool?
and maybe I'm not a fool, I've just lost my mind
because I know better.
When did I keep following a feeling and breathing
in all the smoke screens like one day they'd hand
me the answers?

the most bitter pills to swallow
are the ones no one can know
you have to take down in the
first place.
Choking's hazardous when
circumstances paralyze you
and no one's around to hand
you the water.
you get it down into the pit of
your stomach and it's only then
that you realize
getting it down made the
paralysis powerless
and the only way to survive
circumstance
is acceptance.

secrets

wait out the storm.
just one more second, one more night,
laying in a shrinking room with my
hands glued to my chest.

one more night, every night.
Maybe one day I'll just be
me again.

But for now,
I'll lay in a shrinking room
playing house with demons
that make me forget
i have a voice.

That's the thing about leaving.
There's nothing in this world that made a
selfish man love me more
than when he had to watch me walk away.

in another life
you were
my happily ever after.
but when we arrived here
in the present,
there were a few pieces
that didn't quite fit.

maybe they're out
lost in the cosmos
maybe we just
hadn't found them yet
either way
we couldn't quite make it
through this life
without them.

(and that's okay)

I'm watching you walk away through the rain on my
windowpane, but you're still coming back to me.
Smiling in the nighttime, streetlights and seatcovers
"I wouldn't be me if it weren't for you."

But it doesn't feel like finding eachother,
it feels like letting go.

I'm holding your words
like the doorknob to a dusty doorway in the past,
some days I wish I could go back to feel it all twice, but
mostly I wish that we could go forward,
defy the odds,
forgive,
and make it work.

But I see you laughing in my living room and
sleeping through my sunday afternoons. If you're
the only relic that can stay with me from a past life
I'd choose it a million times over, your hands
locked on my arms,
a kiss cornered with a smile

You always wore your hair in your face,
but I never forget to find what's behind it.

I was naive to think
we would ever work.
naive,
but knowing never
changed the hurt.
You love the shining
edges of the shallow
beginning,
but the accolades of a new lover
don't translate to winning,

and I radiate just as much
with the dull edges
between all my golden
moments.

ALYSSA BURLEY

SPRING 2020

We were looking far ahead and
spelling out the plans as if
every breath and every golden
day between us and the future

were sealed

with the promise of a quiet
invincibility. So much so that
when we forgot our
tomorrows and turned our
eyes towards night skies,
smoke machines and
city lights,
that we neglected to tend to
the possibility
that all our tomorrows were
sealed
and labelled
tallied like objects in a
Kindergarten classroom
and
with the veil of youth and
routine over our eyes,

we were too engrossed with our
own plans to ever pay mind to
the universe that had its own.

and now we stay up until 7am
sinking alone into the bedrooms of our younger years
memories in our heads and
music in our ears
grasping for a string of hope

that could salvage the idea that all our plans weren't so
paper thin.

Life throws you bullet after bullet
teaching you to navigate rocky waters,
and eventually you realize

the best thing about drowning
is learning how to swim.

(excerpt from the journal of a 16 year-old me)

I thought if i fanned the flames i could
love you like that again
and yet i fanned until my arms burned
trying to calm an ache in my chest,
but I suppose i can't call
the hurt I feel
love.
I am torn.
I don't know how to love you.
and selfishly,
I don't know how to let you go.

There's an Expo Marker note on your mirror.
It's in my handwriting, and I know
it'll be gone by morning
the way I usually am from your head.
The other women walking in
might misconstrue the love written there for what it truly is.

I keep holding you close like it's only our cities that separate us, but truly
between us are a million words we'll never say and a common ground so
distant
so deep that it'd take an earthquake to find it.

the spaces between linens and words soaked up in the glow of a july
night's city skyline pull me into the harsh gravity of reality.

I go here all the time,
I've been here in a dream,
I've been here in my mind in the night before I sleep.
in daydreams I'm laughing here in this bed.
But now that I'm here,

It doesn't feel like home quite the way it did in my head.

It's not one color it's all of them when I miss you its
every blended moment and
movement of the sky
and this deep cavern of longing that separates me
from the security of the next time I look you in the
eye.

HELEN

And I knew that you could die, but a mark
like yours would never pass us by.
each generation beyond you will inherit a
bit of your love,
never knowing that it once belonged to you.
A headstone deep in the foothills says that
your stay here came to an end,

Yet somehow I've seen you everywhere the
past two days. You're in the people around
me.
I hear you when i laugh,
and when my dad smiles, and I see you
when I look in the mirror.

and in these seconds I still feel you here,
for this I am grateful beyond any
measurability.
I see you when I see me, I'll see you in my
own babies, and I know,
i'll discover more of you in the world than I
ever imagined,
No matter if you're gone,
what left you was life—
and in life you left your love.

(Excerpt)

You dance through the somedays you dreamed
up as a child and stumble into tomorrows with
new lows for the finding,
Ambiguity can be refreshing when you're sitting
in the gilded chair of your somedays,
but I've found that life is more about what you
do when the sun rises on the days after your
dreams
have passed you by.

If we never talk about it
how will you know?
Forgive me for the space
in my lungs that doesn't
let me speak.

If I can't express love
the only way you know
to read it—
how will you ever know
that I love you?
know that I care?

I pray you understand words
i write in a language
you've never read before.

The holes in my understanding
couldn't be filled with the gaps
in your healing and I'm afraid
I've spent the better part of an eternity
hindering and not helping
your healing.

If I can never say the words
I pray your heart will know
the words I speak in a language foreign to you
say that my love for you will only grow.

Maybe I'll spend each
of my nights laying
in a lonely bed,
convincing myself that I
am worthy enough to breathe
to rest
to sleep.

(or maybe I won't)

The lights turn on when I walk by,
empty basement lovers and a million
reasons why.
I trace my way through the mist of the
day, not thinking of you not thinking
of me somewhere far away,
no longer a soulmate, but a boy that
lit me on fire and swept the ashes away.

I hope there's more to connection than
the muted colors of disappointment and
disappearing— because finding closure
with ghosts and conversations we—I—
didn't know were our last

numbs my heart in a way I pray comes
to pass.

I'll write you poetry and
sit out waiting for you in the rain—
but i'll never tell you you're the only
one.
because I'll let you down.
and saving your expectations
is the only way to save you the pain.

Maybe you already got what you wanted out of me.
Maybe you played with smoke and mirrors so well that even
while it was all a facade,
I'd still trace the pathway of your thumb down my cheek-
bones until we said hello again.

Maybe it wasn't the distance,
forget the space and every limitation the world set out for
us. Maybe you were exactly who everyone said you were
and I claim all of the guilt and none of the reward that
comes with seeing only the romantic parts of someone
sent to teach you a lesson in the painful truth.

Maybe you got what you wanted from me already.
Maybe our string of magic spread out across the past was
enough to make the magnetism of our connection hold
far less gravity to you.

Or maybe you didn't.
Maybe the light is still on in our room in my mind because
you still sit on that golden hill in your mind at night before
you fall asleep.

Maybe somewhere in that fickle head—
there's still a picture on the wall of all the plans we made,
hung with my smile and held by our embrace.

Or maybe you got what you wanted from me already.
Not even the ghost of my smile on the body of every woman
you see held enough strength to bring you back to me.
It's hard to walk a bridge that's half complete, and I'm going
to stop waiting for it to rain right here under
the sea
because you'll only ever choose the limelight
and I'll have to end up choosing me.

you don't call to explain your absence anymore,
you're probably just as well off as you were before.

your face isn't a paperweight on my heart anymore
the time and distance saving me a worn revolving
door.

I can't remember what it felt like for our universes
to collide,
but everytime I drive past that bar my mind is
always inside.

fumbling hands with the artistry and grace of a late
July thunderstorm
a thumb on the doorknob gliding over the questions
that I keep
Toronto holds fast to the whispers of winter but i am
too far too gone to notice their dying touch.
"Will I ever see you again?"
His eyes hardly rise to the brink of goodbye but even
flickering, they find me.
"Its too cold in Toronto this time of year."

And now that I find every moment
reduced to the pros and cons of sharing
that time with you
Every conversation and glance of the eyes
A check in either column,
Adding up arguments and subtracting
smiles
viewing love in terms of assets and not
feeling
While I try to decide whether or not I'm
better off without you.
Each moment so full
It's hard to decide if any of them will
survive
the watchful eye of a woman learning
to move on.

history is a hard mountain to climb
when youre trying
to forgive and forget.

the world is asleep
but here i am
breaking from too much forgetting
and even more
remembering you.

trying to recall every memory is like trying
to grab clouds from the sky but
when it rains it pours
and I'll never forget how much light you brought
to the world
or how much it burned
when we lost you.

If the door is closing and a
part of me is still stuck
inside,
how do I live without the
piece of myself I left in the
life I couldn't love?

A. BURLEY

DAYS WORTH DANCING ABOUT

People tend to speak in cliches and universal blanket terms when giving advice or consoling someone in distress— and LORD— it can feel so painful to hear that sort of truth when the blue of nostalgia or sadness still tints your vision so heavily.

But— it's the blanket terms and universal truths that can pull you out of an emotion so suffocating and remind you how abundant the world out there waiting for you truly is (if you'll let it be).

I'll never forget the sinking feeling in my chest in 2018 when I heard that my recently-deceased grandpa's house had sold. My heart warmed when I caught wind of the new family enjoying the warmth of the rooms my family once graced— but I couldn't help but sink into the fear that the invisble thread connecting my loved ones to me was thinning out. Every moment with them always felt like a gold piece in a barren world, I cherished my time with my loved ones and shot many 11:11 wishes into the void as a child, attempting to alleviate the insufferable distance.

Like lights shining over some forgotten photo album in a weathered attic miles away, I found myself in memories far off, crashing down into the realization that nothing would ever be the same.

Landing in Orange County, California in April of 2019 looked nothing like getting off the exit that led to a million moments with my loved ones in Green Bay, WI. Yet the smile on my Aunt Renee's face when she saw us coming towards her in that airport could've been enough proof of time travel for me to bet my life on it.

Loving every minute of letting the beauty of the San Diego terrain steal the air from my lungs, even then— It hadn't hit me yet.

Of all the events of the trip— the sting ray that tried to steal my foot, the volcano we climbed, the beaches we walked, the desert we hiked— when I think about joy I'm always back in a darkened living room with my aunt Renee, my sister Elaina, and my mom (Nicole, but she's mom to me).

Maybe I'll never remember the songs that played but I'll never forget feeling so undeniably at home in a living room I'd never set foot in before while spinning around with the hands of my family in my own. Smiles spreading from every corner of the room, I felt the pull of a golden string tying me back to a million moments I thought I'd never find again, all through the people I had the privilege of enjoying in that moment.

Cackling like witches and dancing with weightless feet, it hit me then in that living room that the warm light of my grandpa's house would never leave me.
Somehow, despite all my fears I found myself dancing around that California countryside with my family, and I felt whole. I felt that same warm light radiating out of everyone in the room.
So while you're sinking, or maybe just a moment after you've finished falling down a rabbit hole of all your fears— fall back down into that feeling in your chest. The one pulling you towards people and places renting free space in your heart.

It's there you'll find the invisible string, connecting you to everyone you love across thousands of miles and a million little moments. It's then that you'll retreat from your tears and into the embrace of a million universal truths, a billion blanket terms and too many cliches. Scrolling down through that mental inventory, eventually one will melt into your memory.
Everything comes full circle.
Joy comes full circle, and one day when you think all has been lost, you'll wake up to love looking at you on through the glass by your front door, and even if you don't do it—
I'd bet you'll feel like it's a moment worth dancing about.

"... But I'm here now, and i think that means I have to have more faith in possibility rather than thinking it's just some kind of un-attainable dream."
-Mani Marie
(Twitter: @Melanatedmomma)

you are stronger than you were last year,
more yourself too.
yet still in this world
there's a struggle set aside for you.
But you persevere and you
shoulder weight that once threatened
to crush you.
You struggle and you are strong,
and you will persevere.
Because everything you ever needed
to make it through
has always lived
at the core of you

And it'll burn no matter what because
you'll never chase it fast enough,
but perhaps you'll have a night you
become lit so deeply on fire with joy
and adventure that you forget any part
of you ever existed before you sat on
a barstool with giggles bubbling over
your tequila-tinted smile.

Beyond everything,
you were always just one to chase after
the light with your entire life force.

your stars shine by comparison
but someone else's beauty
never made you any less
worthy.

I DON'T KNOW YET

but i never in all my years
anticipated such a sparkling mess
as this
to call my own.

(excerpt from the journal of a 17 year old me)

it makes sense to me now
that my third grade art class showed
me how the complementary colors
are the the opposite ones.
because I think about your small laugh
through a spring nighttime
and I know its a miracle it ever
transcended the time and terrain it took
to be there at all.

but maybe it wasn't
a miracle in the slightest
maybe that glimmer of joy defeated
the odds because
it was meant to.

I look at you and take in that sly grin
and it all makes sense to me now
how the complementary colors
are the opposite ones.

if you can feel in the desensitized world,
you are the lucky one.
in feeling all the depths life has to offer,
you don't place limits on the fullness of
your world—
the possibilities of your heart are
boundless and
although you weep in devastation,
joy shines out from your core when you
find it.
If you can feel in the desensitized world,
you are the lucky one.

I promise.

remembering you comes in golden
flashes
of a RayBan framed face and
how you looked standing in the emerald
waves like a 2002 Kodak daydream with
your hand
in your hair and salt
on your skin.

and there we are poking holes
through the night sky
shining stars in the darkness,
a million moments of you and I

So I'll keep you somewhere quietly
beside my good-will,
next to my hopes and dreams.
Our passing glances will fade,
the days i saved your life
will fade.
But
I know that I always hope that the sun
shining over your days is kind to you,
and that when the time is right—
you find the halls of your memory
smiling kindly back on me.

Years pass
and the pain that used to stalk you
through the night
no longer wakes up with you.

Soak it up,
look over your shoulder
to hindsight and revel in it.
all these insurmountable things
you have survived.

It's hard to believe that someone
who lived through the worst day of
their life is anything less than
unstoppable.

anything less than strong.

If you're feeling unloved and you're doing your best
and you can't for the life of you figure out why it
seems everything's become a mess—
know this.
If you take a puzzle piece from one puzzle and toss
in a different puzzle's box—
it's never going to fit.
Regardless of how important that piece was to the
box it belonged in.
The same goes for people. Your edges and your
talents and quirks are needed desperately
somewhere, so much more than they feel
unneeded
where you are.

You will find your soul circle. You will find the
people
that make you feel like your wandering heart has
arrived at it's destination—
and you will realize it was in the plans all along.
Nobody's meant to suffer forever, just long enough
to figure out where they truly belong.

and just as beautiful clouds
sail over the sea
I might just have the strength
to let you wash over me.

Although 4am in New York is midnight on the
west coast, we find eachother in our subconscious

in our hopes, our dreams, and in our prayers.

I find you in my heart. Years may separate us, and
time may put miles between us, but there's a home
in my heart for everyone I have ever loved,
with the hopes that one day they'll come back to
rest here next to me,
one moment more.

family

Your name no longer burns or brightens my
life.
Today is the someday that I dreamed of
on this day
a year ago.
the passion and the pain have passed me by
and the cycle of heartache forgot to stop at my
doorstep this morning.
It is a task to fill the space I gained when I
kicked you out.

but gratefully
the spaces that exist there are more joyful than
you ever were.

It's time.
You could wait your whole life
with fear or respect drowning out the desire
in your chest,
but dear—
you can't waste all the want in the world
waiting to love someone
because you're afraid to love them imperfectly.

I'd imagine that the daisies from our adolecsent daydream
are still floating down the water of our first summer's day
stream.
Stardust poured from your eyes when you talked about a
place
so far off, but calling your name.

you yearned for it even as you filled my sun-soaked days
with freedom and
adventure.

Years spent in waiting,
and I finally found
my big-city hippie followed
the fire in her heart and ran

all the way home
to the city that never sleeps.

Pause to smile at the mirror
before you smash it.
We all look more beautiful with
stars in our eyes.

A year later and I'm finally
spilling all the blood on the
floor and
healing all the holes in myself
I thought I could board and dry
and deny they were there.

ALYSSA BURLEY

Maybe there's still space in the universe
for a magic I haven't quite touched yet.

an oasis in the raging
storm, today I am
me for the first
time it seems,
in a lifetime.

Battles wait on the
horizon for my arrival,
but today I sit in
the sunshine of possibility—
and gaze at the
glimmers of hope rising
up all around me.

You can save someone's life just by being what you are.

I DON'T KNOW YET

I've been stealing
moments of peace
between storms that
leave me battered
and bruised. How is
it that in my darkest
moments
I've been near the
first people who
never made me
feel used?

(silver linings)

Come back to Earth, they
don't laugh like you up in
the sky— no one else's
smile has filed me into
flight or had me driving so
often through the night.
Rock solid even before we
collided, it's only a faultline
of friendship like ours that
could've ever
made me want to come
back to earth.

give up control and
lay down in the
bitter storm.

If they offered you
a hand, take it.

If they burn you,
feel it.

If you wait your whole life for a better
future and never find it,
one day
winding back through the
moments of your life—
you'll realize that
in all those years you thought you
wasted in waiting for the perfect life,
Life found you.
And 50 years later what you thought
was the space between moments,
looks like living when you see it through
the windows of your memory.

You find life in the spaces between
your golden moments,
lost and confused and devoid of
direction
you just might wander
into something
magic

I have to wear it
on my sleeve now
because my pain is
spelled out across
me in scars like
a red A on my
chest. But maybe
I was always
supposed to wear it
there, to share
and to spare others
the fall into the
isolation that comes
with the shameful
premonition
that you're the
only one whose ever
fallen that far.

ALYSSA BURLEY

I've been looking at the wrong constellations my
entire life,
I realized it then when you were
picking skyscrapers off the skyline like
they could ever accurately depict
how you think of me—

But you see dragons in the pastel sky and pull dreams
from your head like points on a map for the finding

so if I've been looking at the wrong constellations my
entire life
maybe I'll just start picking glowing flecks of the
universe out of the sky
and running so fast towards my dreams
you'd think I could fly.

there may be miles of road ahead of me
but there is an entire
endeavor behind me as well
and I am grateful for the stregnth
I'm just now realizing I
always had in me.

eyes that say yes, I'm living in a dozen different
cascading memories with you,
jumping and falling down every city street into
the magnetism of your smile.

If it's all going to be erased
a few generations down the line
when the titans of our time are no
longer even whispers in the wind,
then let it be written in bold type
and italics,
as if every step you took was magic,
and let it
be magic.
Because if it's all going to be erased
it might as well feel
like magic
when it's written.

My cheeks burn like the happiness
in my gut and if I could choose my forever
it'd be this second
if I could choose my forever
I'd pick that feeling
I'd pick those people
I'd choose those moments.
Falling away from forever
I'll watch my life rotate
into dust,
But if I could stop the clock
I'd swear I couldn't hesitate
I'd choose today.
Because the morning after forever
was the worst morning
of my life.

that's just it.
you don't have to know, and
the chances are— you never
will.

Even when you stand with so
much confidence and
conviction, with so much
faith in your knowledge you'd
bet your life on it—
even *then.*

You don't have to have any
certainty in anything except
your ability to make magic
out of the most miserable
situations.

You're allowed to laugh at
yourself and honestly, you'll
be better for it.

every season brings you a
new cross to bear,

but it'll also bring you new
days in the sun.

I pray your days in the sun
balance out every obstacle
you undertake.
Surrender to the unknown,
life starts past your comfort
zone.

I used to get up before school,
lay beneath my covers in the dark and watch the colors of the morning sun
lay waste to the darkness of the night.

At 17, I knew how to heal my heart, and I did a lot of things wrong, but
mostly, I did a few things right.

I'd walk out into the crisp air of a November morning and let the clarity of
the cold wash over me while I pretended that warming up my car was more
of a reason for me to step outside than the awed perception and quiet
healing that comes from observing cosmic color fading out our view of the
universe into the harsh reality of the day.

I did a few things wrong.

I'm sure as I deal with the remaining wreckage spurred by mistakes and
adolescent suburban perception—
I'll hinder portions of my healing that I'll one day have to stare down in the
mirror and sit with like I have so much recently. But beyond the error that
led me to breakage and the burnt nerve endings of my mind—
I knew how to feed the soul. I knew to follow my arrow when all the ashes
of my identity were crashing down at my feet. All there was left to do was
sit in the blazing embers of the past and feel the legnths and widths of
gratitude and despair and
follow the little voice that led me to sights and feelings that handed me a
roadmap to
connectivity and comfort.
If every moment of my life fails me, if the fabric of my being just won't
mend or stitch or fit the guidelines for walking this existential runway, I
know I'll find the Coastline at the edge of my tears, beyond everything I lay
my faith in, and beyond the edges of my being and fears.

What has existed before I knew I was supposed to be anything at all
will always be there, and even if I never find healing how the world will
have you want it,
I'll awe myself at the sparkling waters of a midnight ocean and forget my
fears and ailments in the lilac light of the morning sun—

and I'll heal.
Not in textbook definitions or guidelines of health and normalcy,
I'll heal because we are all more than every construct of the mind and every
moment that became a monstrosity. If I never see beauty in my reflection, I'll
see beauty in the infinite way of the universe and the fact that each of our souls
will outlive the moments in our lives that threaten to keep us down.

So i'll do the same when I fall flat on my face at 27 that I did at 17.

I'll step out and start my car in the freezing frost of the early winter, and I won't
fight the cold. I'll let it seep in all my cracks, caverns, and edges,

and its then. When I'm wide open and invaded with cold vulnerability that
the beauty of the world will fill me up and all my cracks and force me to forget
myself long enough

to thaw me out.

ALYSSA BURLEY

There are so many ways to find yourself,
so many words to frame your face,
and half the time you'll find
you could pour out the dictionary and it
still couldn't completely
capture the essence of your grace.

Beyond the mistakes,
the moments
the pain and the triumph...
who am I?
what fills me up with fire and light?
what do I dream about?

After stripping away the past, and all my attachments,
painfully and beautifully existing
immersed
in the present:

Where am I going?

I used to think I didnt know...

...But maybe I do

the sequel collection
by Alyssa Burley
Coming soon

(above photo by Claudia Gomez - On instagram @ClaudiaGomezphotoz)

Follow @alyssaburley on instagram, @alyssaburley7 on TikTok, and @Lyssaliz for giveaways, new releases, community discussions & more!

Please reach out to me, let's talk writing, music, life, partnership and publishing!

"... beautiful and inspiring. It makes me want to run, reach out to others, reach out to my younger self, reach out to my older self with hope, inspiration, wanderlust, and hope. Thank you [Alyssa] for making this and listening to your creative impulses... I just realized I said hope twice. That's how powerful it is."
—Dr. Angela Jann, Professor of the Arts, Capital University.

"wow this book is pretty cool."
—my mom after seeing the book for the first time

From Me:
    This book was so far out of my comfort zone it's not even funny in the slightest. It's intense where I like to laugh at intensity, heartfelt where I'd been more comfortable being lesser so. But in the end I am just as much the deepest, uncomfortable parts of me as i am the lightest and most inviting. WOW! This journey has been exhilirating, and I am beyond grateful. For a girl that used to put little padlocks on her notebooks as a kid, this is a plot twist. I hope you enjoyed.

if you made it to this page, thank you. I am so grateful for you.